# Ants

*Amazing Facts & Pictures for Children on These Amazing Creatures*

**(Awesome Creature Series)**

By Hathai Ross

# Table of Contents

# Introduction

Thank you for downloading this book.

Ants are crawling creatures that are so fascinating. They may be little but they sure are not insignificant. Their life is a huge mine of fascinating facts. Ants can live anywhere and can practically eat anything.

Learn more about ants in this book. Here, you will learn:

- Amazing facts about the different types of ants

- Life in the ant colony

- The different members of the colony and their different roles

- The diet of ants and how they eat

- The areas where different kinds of ants like to live

- And so much more

Read this book today and you will also learn a few more things about some of the notable ants like:

- Red fire ants

- Argentine ants

- Crazy ants

- Odorous house ants

- Pavement ants

- Carpenter ants

Read this book today and see how amazing these creatures are!

# Chapter 1: The Wonderful Life of Ants

Ants are found in practically every corner of the world, except the icy cold land of Antarctica. Ant species add up to more than 12,000. These small creatures have been around for millions of years. They live in various nooks and crannies, in just about anywhere they can crawl into.

A lot of people treat ants as pests. They get into homes and build their colonies. They always try to get to your food and can be pesky during picnics. Nature has use for these ants. They are social insects that live in large groups, called colonies. Each colony can have as many as several millions of ants.

## The Colonies

Ants build colonies in all shapes and sizes and in every space they can crawl into. The size varies from a small one that only contains a few dozen. An average colony has several thousands of ants. Small ant colonies often create their nests within cracks or crevices. Larger colonies build huge nests. Ants in large colonies need to forage (search far and wide) for food and supplies. There are even larger ones, called super colonies. There are about 300 million individual ants and more in these vast colonies. Super colonies have been found in Australia, southern Europe, Japan and the United States.

As social insects, ants have designated roles in the colony, each role is important in maintaining the colony. In a colony, there are 3 types of ants. There is the queen ant, the workers ants and the males.

### *The Queen Ant*

The queen lives a long life and gives birth to millions of baby ants throughout her life. She is the only one who can lay eggs that hatch into baby ants. She is the largest ant in the colony.

She also has wings. The wings are shed when starting a new nest. If the queen dies, the colony will only survive for a few months. The queen is rarely replaced. Also, worker ants cannot reproduce and be the next queen. Ant colonies may have 1 or more queens, depending on the species (kind).

### The Male Ants

The male ants also have wings. Their only job is to fertilize ants that may become a queen one day. After they mate, the male ants die. They have no other role in the colony other than mating.

## The Worker Ants

Only the worker ants do not have wings. Worker ants are all the other females in the colony. Their responsibilities include feeding the larvae or baby ants. They are also responsible in taking out trash from the colony. Worker ants are also the ones who goout and search for supplies and food. They are also in charge in defending the colony against attackers.

### *The Soldiers*

Each ant colony has soldier ants. They protect the queen, gather or hunt for food, defend the colony or attack other ant colonies for food and for more nesting space.

If the soldier ants defeat another ant colony, all the eggs of the losing colony are taken away. These are hatched in the winning colony. Once hatched, these ants become "slave ants". They become in charge of taking care of the colony's eggs and baby ants, building ant hills and in gathering more food.

Not all ants build colonies. Some ants, called the army ants, do not have their own nests or homes. They live life in 2 phases, the nomad phase and the stationary phase.

In the nomad phase, the army ants travel the entire day while they attack any colony or other insects they come across for food. They build a temporary nest at night where they rest. The next morning, army ants leave this nest and travel again.

When they enter he stationary phase of their life, their queen lays her eggs. The rest of the colony will stay and wait for these eggs to hatch. The worker army ants make a nest with their bodies to serve as protection for the queen, her eggs and their food.

# AMAZING FACTS

Some of the most unique and notable things about ants are:

- Ants are very strong. They can carry things that are 20 times their body weight. If an ant was a second grader, he can easily carry something as large as a car.

- Ants have no ears. They "hear" through the vibrations that their feet feel coming from the ground.

- Ants do not have any lungs. They breathe through the tiny holes found all over their body.

- Ants fight until one or both of them dies.

- Ever wondered why ants crawl in lines? It's because they are following the trail of pheromone that ants who went foraging previously.

- There are special sensors in the ants' feet that help them gather and understand information from the vibrations in the ground. Hairs and antennae also help in gathering information while they are searching for food.

- There is one type (species) of ant that is all-female, the *M. smithii*. So far, researchers have not yet seen any males of this ant species. The queen clones herself when she reproduces. This ant species is found in Central America and South America.

- Ants can turn into zombies. That is, when they are infected with a certain fungi, which takes over their bodies. The fungi grow and enter the ant's exoskeleton (tough outer cover of their bodies) and then eat the soft tissues inside. Then, the ant will find a leaf and bites it (death grip), never letting go until he dies. The fungi will then release its spores into the air and infect other ants.

- There are 1 million ants for every human on earth. That's how many these small, amazing insects are.

# Chapter 2: Argentine Ants

The Argentine ant is invincible. This is considered as the number 1 nuisance in the United States.

## What do Argentine Ants look like?

They are among the most recognizable ant species. They have massive sizes compared to other ant species. They grow to an average of 2 to 3 millimeters long (1/16th of an inch to 1/14th). They have 6 legs. Some Argentine ants have wings while some don't.

Argentine ants are deep brown to black in color. Queen ants and male ants are slightly larger than the rest of the colony. Their colors are also darker.

The mandibles of Argentine ants are lined with 5 to 8 large teeth. The eyes are positioned below the head's widest point. The long antenna has 12 segments. The thorax and the abdomen are separated by a single node. The ant's body is smooth and shiny, without any hair at the back of the thorax and head. They have no sting but that does not mean they do not bite. Their bite is pretty nasty.

## Where do Argentine ants live?

These ants are native species in Argentina (hence the name) and Brazil. In the last few years, they are also found in southeastern portion of the United States such as in Washington, Oregon, California, Missouri, Illinois and Maryland. They are now living in 16 countries all over the world. These are believed to be introduced in the US in the 1890s by freight ships.

They live in both dry and moist environments. They can build their colonies beneath wood, mulch or debris. They can also build their nests in the soil or in the holes at the base of trees and shrubs.

Colonies are typically in wet places and close to their food source. Argentine ants are not harmful to human health. However, their droppings (feces) can contaminate food. When crushed, Argentine ants emit a foul odor.

They are renowned for the super-sized colonies they build when given the chance. They breed fast and in huge numbers. Their colonies can grow to immense sizes. Sometimes, if they get the chance, Argentine ant colonies can cover an entire garden or backyard. This is one of the reasons why they are considered as the most annoying pest in the US.

Argentine ants are very aggressive. They are known to keep attacking colonies of other ant species. They have also been observed to join forces with other Argentine ant colonies and unite in their attacks against weaker enemy colonies.

There are usually hundreds of queens in a single Argentine ant colony. This is one of the reasons why the colonies can grow to very large sizes. The colonies expand not by swarming or taking over other ant's colonies. Instead, the Argentine ant colony is expanded by creating new nests near and around the old colony. New nests remain connected to the old colony. Each colony has millions of ants with several queens. Together, these ants can easily populate one entire city block.

## What do they eat?

Argentine ants prefer sweet food but they are also known for eating almost anything, such as oils, fats, eggs and meats. They usually go for sweets like fruit juices, syrup and plant secretions. They also keep aphids in their colonies because they love to eat the aphid's sugary secretions. Argentine ants bite off the aphids' wings to prevent them from flying away.

When Argentine ants search for food, they leave several trails of pheromones all over the place and not just from their nest and directly to the food. They do this to save time by not having to visit the same area twice. When these ants travel, they leave wide pheromone trails. These trails have lanes that are as wide as 3-5 ants held side by side.

Other kinds of ants only have the worker ants to search for food. With Argentine ants, the queen also helps in searching for food.

# Chapter 3: Pavement Ants

Like the name suggests, pavement ants are those that live in between the cracks and lines of pavements.

## What do pavement ants look like?

Pavement ants range from deep brown color to black. They grow to about 1/8 to 1/16 of an inch long. The bodies are oval and are segmented. They are dark brown to black. Their 6 legs are paler in color. Their antennae are also paler than the rest of the body.

Pavements ants have a pair of spines located on their backs. There are grooves present on their heads and thorax. The antennae has 12 segments, with the club (free end of the antennae) further divided into 3 segments. A stinger is present at the last segment in the pavement ant's abdomen.

## Where do they live?

They can be seen all over the United States, especially in the eastern half of the country. They are not harmful to human health but they can contaminate food by leaving their droppings.

Pavement ants are believed to have reached the United States via the European merchant vessels in the 1700s to 1800s. These merchant ships were often filled with soil in order to add weight for overseas voyage. These soils are believed to have carried pavement ants. Upon arriving at the port, the soil was removed and then replaced with trade goods.

Pavement ants can live inside homes but they are most commonly the kind that lives under pavements. They also build their colonies under the sidewalk, slabs, driveways and patios. They are the ones responsible for the piles of fine dirt on top of pavements. They are familiar in the summer months, when people could see a lot of mounds of dirt piles on pavement cracks, in driveways, on the floor near walls, patios and sidewalks. When they choose to build their nests indoors, pavement ants usually pick the building's foundation as their mains site. Indoors, they build their colonies under the floors and within walls. As they grow in number and expand their colony, they also hollow out the building's foundation walls. Colonies have about 3,000-4,000 ants living in it. The colonies also have several queens.

# What do pavement ants eat?

These ants can eat almost anything. They are not picky eaters. They eat seeds, bread, grease, other insects, honey, honeydew (from aphids, other insects, seeds, nectar and fruits), cheese, nuts, meats- everything they can get.

When pavement ants go out to find food, they invade buildings and homes. They can often be seen crawling in wiggly lines along walls and corners carrying eggs, food, excavated debris or soil from one pavement ant colony to another.

They can be of concern when they come in swarms inside garden patios or kitchens in search for and to collect food.

## The Colonies

When a queen pavement ant lays her eggs, a new colony is formed. Worker pavement ants take care of these eggs. They transfer these eggs and any newly hatched larvae to another colony in order to avoid any changes in the moisture and temperature that can affect them.

They are found in larger colonies in the West Coast and Midwest, and along the coastal region of the Atlantic. They are also found in the southern states up to the mid-Atlantic states.

# Chapter 4: Carpenter Ants

Carpenter ants are among the most common indoor ants. They do not eat wood like termites but can still cause a lot of damage to houses. They dig tunnels and build their nets within the wooden structures of the house. This can cause accelerated degradation of the lumber parts of the house. These ants also prefer building their nests or colonies in damp wood, which earned them the name "carpenter ants".

## What do carpenter ants look like?

Carpenter ants vary in size. Worker ants generally grow to about ¼ of an inch, which is about the width of a regular pencil. Queen carpenter ants grow larger, at ¾ of an inch. This is roughly the size of a quarter. The average length of this ant is about 5/8 of an inch. They have 6 legs. Worker carpenter ants are the only ones that do not have any wings and their bodies are black in color. They also have a pair of antenna on their heads.

The body of the carpenter ant is oval. The color varies from red to black. Carpenter ants are among the large kinds of ants. Their size makes them look threatening. Their colors differ depending on what species or kind of carpenter ants. The black carpenter ants are more common. Other kinds of carpenter ants have colors ranging from yellow to red.

They have a single node found between their abdomen and the thorax. The ant's thorax is smooth and uniformly round. The thorax looks arched when seen from the side. At the tip of the abdomen is a ring of hair. Worker carpenter ants have larger mandibles or jaws compared to others.

Often, carpenter ants are confused with termites. They generally have the same large, black bodies and both live in wood. Look closely to see they there are obvious differences between them. Carpenter ants have narrow waists and their antennae are bent. If present, the lower or hind wings are smaller than the ones in front.

## Where do carpenter ants live?

Carpenter ants build their colonies in places where there is damp or moldy wood, with a good water source nearby. This includes tree stumps, in the plants or in firewood. Usually, carpenter ants build nests inside buildings, in places where there is water

leakage or when there are woody places that have become wet and damaged. However, there are also some colonies in dry environments.

When they establish their nests in the wooden parts of a house or building, they ruin it. These ants build smooth tunnels within the wood, which weakens the structure.

# What do carpenter ants eat?

Carpenter ants live in wood but do not eat it. They remove portions of wood to expand their colonies. That is why there are small mounds of tiny wood pieces that line the entrance to their colonies. These small piles of wood are called frass.

What they eat are other insects (alive or dead), fats, and meats. They also love sugary foods, including nectar and honeydew (sweet and sticky fluid that aphids leave behind). They also eat fruits and plant juices, as well as pet food.

## *The Colonies*

Each carpenter ant colony has one queen. She builds her nest within a cavity or crack in the wood. Here, she lays the first batch of eggs that will hatch into workers. Once the eggs hatch, she feeds the larvae with her own saliva. The queen never leaves the nest or eats anything while she takes care of her babies.

Once they are old enough, the worker carpenter ants go out of the nest in search for food. The queen will then lay the 2nd batch or generation of ants in the colony. Food gathered by the first generation worker ants will feed the next generation. Population of carpenter ant colonies grow very fast. One colony can have as much as 2,000 worker ants and more.

# Chapter 5: Odorous House Ants

Odorous house ants are known for the stinky odor they produce when their nests are attacked. They also produce the stinky smell when they are crushed. This smell is meant to drive animals that want to eat them or destroy their home. The smell is similar to the smell of rotten coconuts or old butter. But, despite the word "house" in their names, they live mostly outside. When they enter a house, it's mostly to find food.

## What odorous house ants look like?

Odorous house ants can grow from 1/16<sup>th</sup> to 1/8 of an inch or 2.4 mm to 3.25 mm long. The shape of their bodies is oval, uneven and segmented. Their colors are either black or brown. They have 6 legs and a pair of antennae. Some odorous house ants have wings while some don't.

## Where odorous ants live

These ants are native to the US, found all throughout the country. Each colony can have as many as 100,000 individual ants.

Odorous house ants live long lives. They can live both indoors and outdoors, although they usually build their colonies in exposed soil. They also like to build their nests under debris, mulch, logs, stones or other things. They also build their homes in cracks on the floor and walls. They prefer to build homes outdoors but tend to move their colonies indoors during fall season or rainy weather. Inside the house, odorous house ants build their homes within cracks in the wall near heaters and hot water pipes. They also build their nests behind the cabinets, under the floor or under the sink.

## What do odorous house ants eat

Odorous house ants are often seen travelling in long trails. They look for food all day and even at night. These ants like sugary sweet foods they can find outdoors, most especially melons. They also eat honeydew, the sweet liquid waste of aphids. They also eat dead insects. They practically eat anything, including plant secretions and seeds.

Inside the house, they will eat meats, pastries, dairy products, sweets, fruit juices, vegetables (raw or cooked) and grease. When looking for food inside the house, these odorous house ants will make trails along sinks, cabinets, baseboards and kitchen counters.

### *The Colonies*

Odorous house ants can build colonies in varying sizes. Some colonies can have hundreds of worker ants with only one queen. Some can be very large, consisting of thousands of worker ants with hundreds of queens all in the same vast colony. Queens can lay so many eggs that will hatch into thousands of worker ants and hundreds of fertile ants (ants that can mate and lay many eggs).

# Chapter 6:
# Fire Ants

Fire ants are known by many other names. They are also called RIFA or red imported fire ants, red fire ants or simply fire ants. Unlike the other ants previously discussed, red fire ants are more aggressive. They are well known for their very painful sting. Once they are threatened, they will bite and hold on with their jaws. They will then thrust their stinger into the victim, either a human or other animals. They will inject their venom, which causes a burning sensation that can be very painful. When stung, a raised welt appears and then turns into a white blister or pustules, which are also very itchy. People who have sting allergy will have more serious reactions.

Their easily identifiable mounds should be avoided. These are amazing ants because they can adapt to changing environments. One great, amazing example is when their home gets flooded. Fire ants come together to form a huge ball. They cannot swim but together, they can build a bridge over the water so each of them can cross. They are also known for coming together and float like a raft!

## What do red fire ants look like?

Fire ants can grow from 1/8- 3/8 of an inch. Their bodies are oval shaped and segmented into 3 parts. The color is a dark, reddish brown to black hue, not really red as their name says.

They have 6 legs and a pair of antennae. Their heads are round and have a copper color. They have an abdominal stinger that they use when threatened.

## Where do red fire ants live?

Red fire ants are not native to the United States. They were accidentally brought into the country through one of the ports in Mobile, Alabama. The imported fire ants were believed to be from South America, on board a cargo shipment in the 1930s. From that time, these ferocious ants marched their way all over the southern portion of the United States, from Florida all the way to California. They also found their way to the north, to Oklahoma and the Virginia.

They like to build their homes in warm and sunny areas such as in the fields, lawns, parks and pastures. Rotting logs, stumps and trees are places where red fire ants also establish their homes. They are also commonly seen building their colonies near the foundation of buildings or in landscape areas.

Red fire ants build their homes outdoors in mounds of soil. They create the recognizable tall dirt mounds that can reach up to 2 feet high above the ground and then up to 3 feet deep into the ground. The tunnels they make are close to the ground surface. They use these tunnels when they search for food. When the weather gets too hot and dry, red fire ants crawl deeper into the ground. When they do, the dirt mounds above the ground will start to shrink.

## What do red fire ants eat?

Red imported fire ants are very greedy eaters. They can easily eat every part of the plant, like the fruits, buds, seeds and leaves. This is why they are not only well known for their painful sting but for their ability to destroy crops and landscapes.

They eat anything. They are omnivores; they eat both meat and plants. Their meal consists of meats, earthworms, spiders, dead animals, ticks, seeds, greasy foods, nectar, sweets and honeydew. They are also known for hunting or killing other insects and other small animals so that the colony will have food to eat.

## *The Colonies*

In an average colony, there could be as many as 10,000 red fire worker ants. Imported fire ants may reach more than 500,000 worker ants in one colony alone. When males and females with wings reproduce, they fly high up in the air and mate. Red fire ants usually mate when the environmental temperature is 70° to 95°, within 24 hours after it rains. After they have mated, the females fly back to the ground and lose their wings. They crawl and look for a new place to make their own colonies. The males die right after they mate, dropping to the ground.

The colony is very protective of their home. They can sense the vibrations in the ground, which warn them if humans or other animals (pets, wildlife, livestock, etc) are approaching their nest. When their colony is disturbed, red fire ants come out by the thousands. They will swarm the intruder and sting him several times.

# Chapter 7: Crazy Ants

Crazy ants are given this name because they run in all directions, like someone crazy. They are not like the other ants that crawl in orderly lines going to a specific direction. Crazy ants seem as if they are just running around without any specific place to go to. They are called by other names, such as rasberry crazy ants (from the exterminator Tom Rasberry who first noticed their growing population in 2002, in the state of Texas), tawny crazy ants and hairy crazy ants.

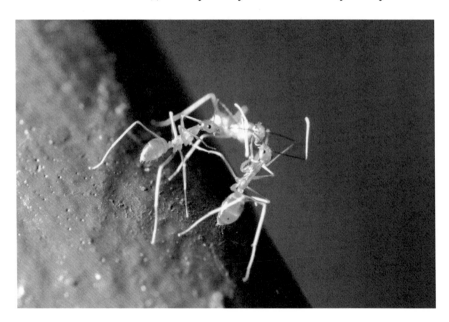

# What do crazy ants look like?

Their most notable feature is the way they move around- in crazy, rapid and erratic movements. The body is reddish brown in color. Their bodies are covered in rough hair. They are small, growing to about 1/8 inch long.

Both male and female crazy ants have wings. However, males do not usually fly. The females lose their wings after they have mated.

At the end of their abdomen, an acidophore is present. This is a small and round opening where venom is released. This acidophore is encircled by a ring of hair. Crazy ants do not have any stingers but they have venom. To put their venom into a person or animals, the crazy ant bites and then curls his body to release and inject his venom.

Their legs are extremely long, compared to most other kinds of ants. Their antennae are also long, segmented into 1 to 2 parts and have no club. The adults are brown to black-colored with a hint of blue tint.

# Where do crazy ants live?

Crazy ants mostly live in the southern portion of the United States. They are especially seen in states along the Gulf Coast, such as Florida, Alabama, Mississippi, Louisiana and Texas. There are also crazy ant colonies up in Massachusetts and New York, as towards the west such as California and Hawaii.

Crazy ants can live in both wet and dry places. They cannot survive very cold temperatures. When the weather becomes too cold outside, they transfer indoors. Unlike other ants, crazy ants do not build nests. Instead, they live right underneath tree cavities, yard waste, inside electronic equipment, and in the soil under stones or trash.

They usually invade people's homes and cause lots of trouble. They make their nest in the soil of potted plants. They crawl everywhere. They even crawl into the coolest openings in electronic gadgets and then cause a short circuit.

### The Colonies

They are very invasive. They come in swarms in a short time and build homes just about everywhere. When crazy ants enter a home, they'd immediately colonize every available space. They also reproduce so fast that in no time, they'd have a dense population over a huge area.

What is really amazing about the crazy ants is that they are attracted to electronic gadgets. Crazy ants are just about the only kind of ants that always find their way into electrical equipment. Their presence in these gadgets causes short circuits. In fact, every year, the damage these crazy ants do to electronics can reach to more than $146 million. The electrical damage starts with one or a few ants getting inside the gadget or electrical equipment. This will cause a short circuit as they get electrocuted. The electrocuted ant/s release pheromones that call to other crazy ants, seeking help. More crazy ants will come to "rescue" and fight the "attacker". As more ants enter the equipment or gadget, more serious damage happens. More ants get electrocuted and more pheromones will be released. The cycle continues. The dead ants pile up inside the electronic gadget and will eventually short out the entire electrical system.

Crazy ant colonies are usually small. Amazingly, each colony has several queens that reproduce rapidly and lay lots of eggs. A colony under a rock 12 inches in diameter will have at least 20 queens, each continually reproducing and laying eggs. Crazy ants are also known to join one colony with another, forming a super colony. Their populations can easily increase from a few thousands to as much as hundreds of millions.

Crazy ants can travel long distances in search for food. They rapidly crawl and look randomly for any food. Worker ants feed on both animals and plants (called omnivorous). They eat living and dead insects. They also eat honeydew, plant secretions, seeds and fruits. They also eat any food they find inside homes such as liquids, grease, produces, meats and sweets.

# Conclusion

Thank you again for downloading this book!

I hope you enjoyed reading about my book on ants. I hope you were able to learn more about a few of the notable species, especially the ones that live close to humans. These are amazing little creatures that must be respected and appreciated. Best of all, you should learn to stay away from them, especially ones that can really give nasty bites like the fire ants. I hope that after reading this book, you will at ants in a whole new perspective- with awe, appreciation and respect.

Finally, if you enjoyed this book, please take the time to share your thoughts and **post a review on Amazon**. It'd be greatly appreciated!

Thank you!

# A Note about The Author

Hathai Ross was born in Thailand and then moved to England in late 2004. She has been writing Books for the past 3 years, mainly on Animals which are her passion.

Feel free to contact Hathai at greenslopesdirect@gmail.com

Check out her Amazon profile here: Hathai Ross

# Next Steps

Write me an honest review about the book – I truly value your opinion and thoughts and I will incorporate them into my next book, which is already underway.

**Leave your review of my Book    Click Here Please**

# Check Out My Other Books

Go ahead and click on the links below to check out the other great books I've published!

**Snakes: Amazing Facts about Snakes with Pictures for Kids**

**Dolphins: Amazing Facts about Dolphins with Pictures for Kids**

**Whales: Amazing Facts about Whales with Pictures for Kids**

**Sharks: Amazing Facts about Sharks with Pictures for Kids:**

**Dinosaurs: Amazing Facts & Pictures for Children On These Wonderful Creatures**

Made in the USA
San Bernardino, CA
26 November 2017